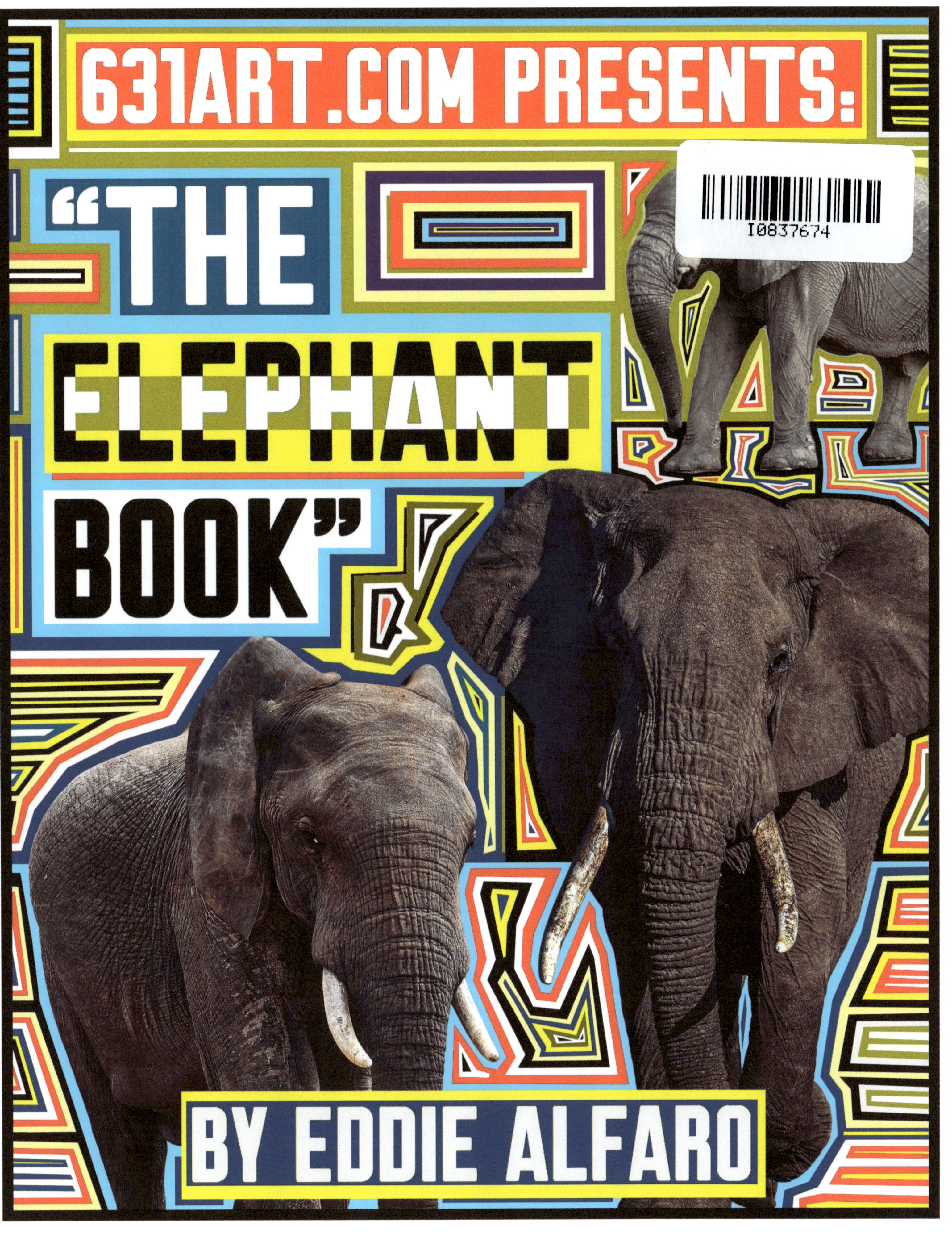
631ART.COM PRESENTS:
"THE ELEPHANT BOOK"
BY EDDIE ALFARO

AN ELEPHANT CAN SMELL WATER UP TO 3 MILES AWAY.

EARS ARE THE EASIEST WAY TO
TELL ELEPHANT SPECIES APART.

AFRICAN ELEPHANTS ARE THE
LARGEST LAND MAMMALS.

ELEPHANTS ARE
HERBIVORES, EATING
A DIET OF GRASS,
FRUIT, LEAVES, TWIGS,
AND TREE BARK.

THE ELEPHANT SPIRIT ANIMAL
SYMBOLIZES STRENGTH AND POWER.

ELEPHANTS ARE SMART, EMOTIONAL,
SELF-AWARE AND HIGHLY SOCIAL CREATURES.

ELEPHANTS USE THEIR BODY, HEAD, EYES,
MOUTH, EARS, TUSKS, TRUNK, TAIL AND
FEET TO COMMUNICATE WITH EACH
OTHER AND OTHER SPECIES.

THE EARS OF AN AFRICAN ELEPHANTS CAN
REACH UP TO 5 FEET LONG.

ELEPHANTS ARE KNOWN FOR
THEIR INCREDIBLE MEMORY.

ELEPHANTS ARE SENSITIVE AND COMPLEX SOCIAL
ANIMALS WHO SEEK THE COMPANIONSHIP OF
OTHER ELEPHANTS, PREFERABLY THEIR OWN FAMILIES.

ELEPHANTS HAVE THE LONGEST GESTATION
PERIOD OF ALL ANIMALS AT 22 MONTHS.

ELEPHANTS WILL WALK AT THE PACE OF THEIR
SLOWEST MEMBER, WITH INFANTS SURROUNDED
BY NURTURING MEMBERS OF THE HERD.

ELEPHANTS LIVE IN HERDS, WHICH ARE HIGHLY ORGANIZED
SOCIAL GROUPS OF 6-20 ELEPHANTS LED AND GUIDED BY AN
OLDER FEMALE LEADER, CALLED A MATRIARCH.

A MATRIARCH WILL MAKE ALL THE DECISIONS FOR THE HERD, INCLUDING WHAT TO EAT, WHERE TO SLEEP AND WHERE TO GO.

FEMALE ELEPHANTS STAY WITH THE
HERD FOR THEIR ENTIRE LIVES.

ELEPHANTS ARE A KEY STONE SPECIES, WHICH MEANS WITHOUT THEM, ENTIRE ECOSYSTEMS WOULD BE DRAMATICALLY DIFFERENT OR CEASE TO EXIST.

ELEPHANTS CAN HEAR EACH OTHER
AS MUCH AS SIX MILES AWAY.

FUN FACTS ABOUT ELEPHANTS:
ELEPHANTS HAVE AROUND 150,000 MUSCLE UNITS IN THEIR TRUNK.
ELEPHANTS USE THEIR TRUNKS TO SUCK UP WATER TO DRINK, IT CAN CONTAIN UP TO TWO GALLONS OF WATER.

ELEPHANT TUSKS ARE ACTUALLY ENLARGED INCISOR TEETH.
AN ELEPHANT'S SKIN IS 1 INCH THICK IN MOST PLACES.
ELEPHANTS NEED UP TO 300 LB. OF FOOD PER DAY.

ELEPHANTS CAN COMMUNICATE THROUGH SEISMIC SIGNALS, SOUNDS THAT CREATE VIBRATIONS IN THE GROUND, THAT THEY CAN DETECT THROUGH THEIR BONES.
ELEPHANT CALVES ARE ABLE TO STAND WITHIN 20 MINUTES OF BEING BORN AND CAN WALK WITHIN 1 HOUR.
AN ELEPHANT'S TRUNK WEIGHS 400 POUNDS, BUT CAN PICK UP THINGS AS SMALL AS A SINGLE GRAIN OF RICE.

THANK YOU.
THE END.

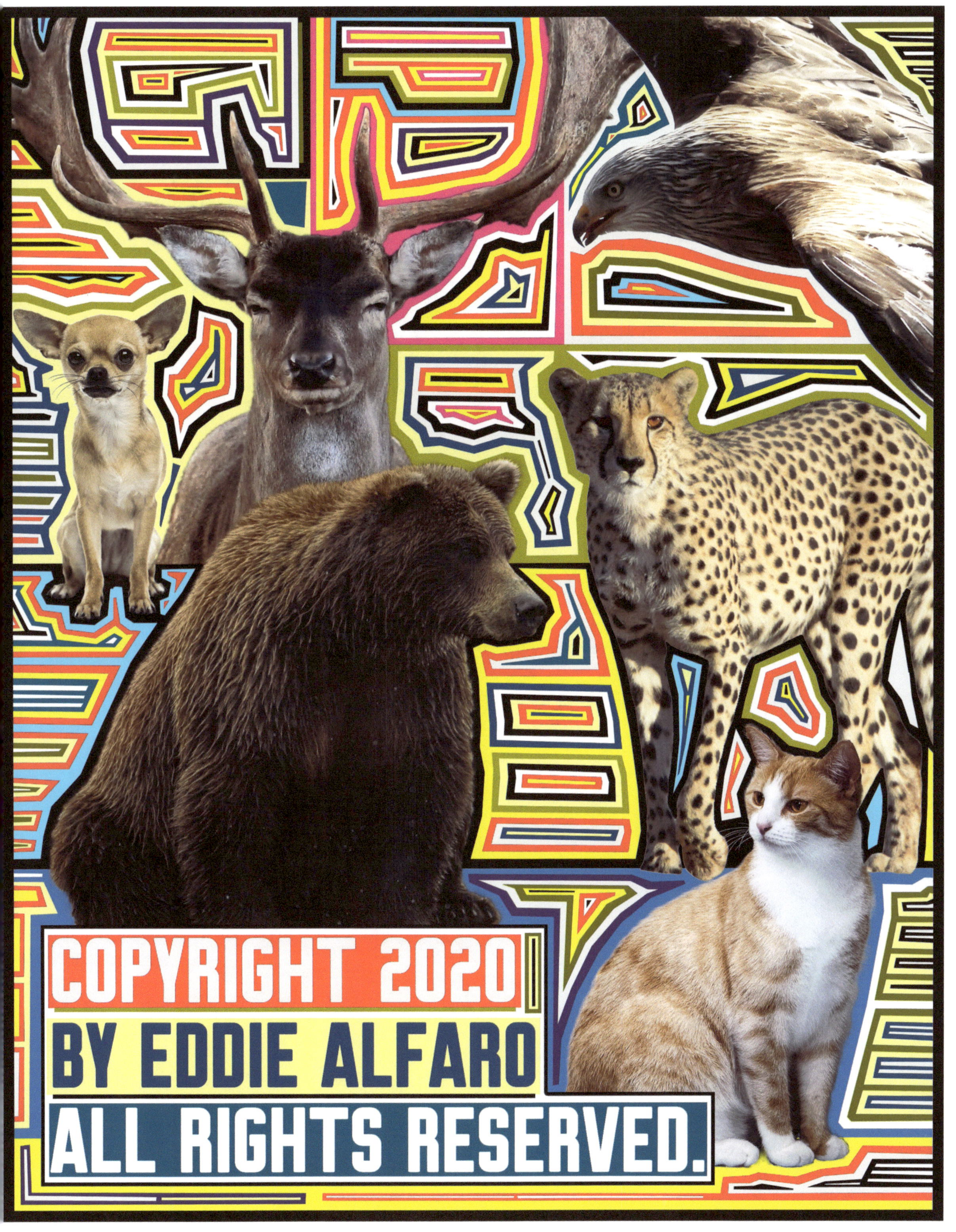

COPYRIGHT 2020
BY EDDIE ALFARO
ALL RIGHTS RESERVED.

MORE BOOKS AT:

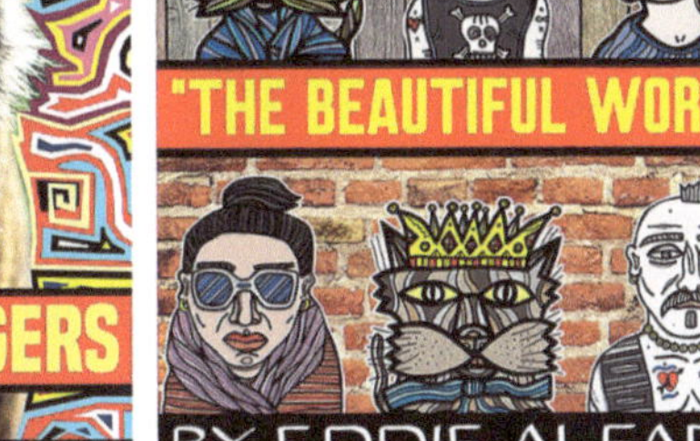

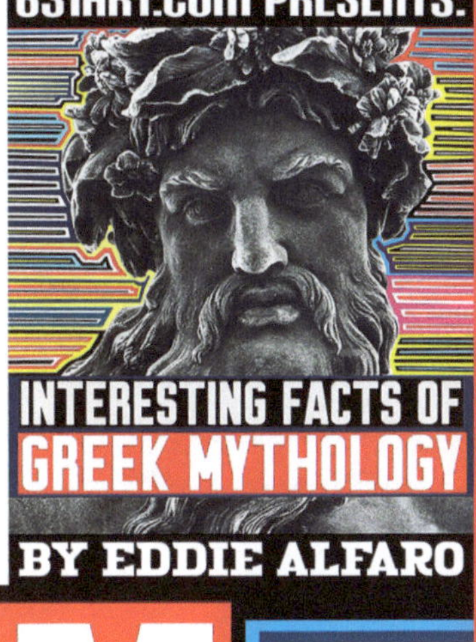

631ART.COM

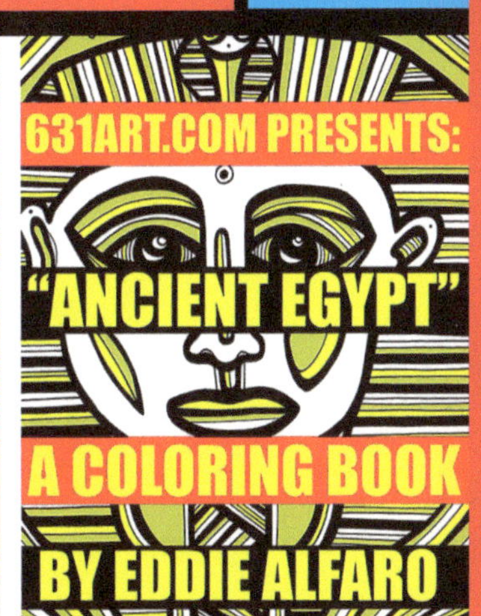